This book started off as a journal. I began writing my thoughts and experiences in hopes that one day I would look back and say, "I MADE IT!"

As a mom, you feel the pressure to be a 'Super Mom.' Not only from society, but from yourself. You push yourself to compete with your inner self, to not have any faults as a mother, to not make any mistakes,
… To be perfect.

You do not want to look inexperienced and you do not want to feel a failure. You want others to look at you and automatically know, "She is a FANTASTIC mother!"
You give yourself a headache from not wanting to let your children down, your own mother, your husband, and more importantly-- you do not want to let yourself down.

You stress yourself to make sure you measure up with other mothers around you, not knowing that these same mothers are feeling the exact things that you are. They look to you in the same light.

Believe it or not, as mothers, we all experience extremely similar thoughts, identical emotions, comparable pressures, and the same *need* to be the best Super Mom we can be.

NOTE: I'm NO pro at being a mom, but I am a pro at being a first time mom ☺

No Nannies Allowed:

A Real Mom's Guide to Being a Real Mom

by: L. M. Wilson

For more information, visit the Mommy's Today website:
http://www.mommystoday.com

Contact: mommystoday@gmail.com

ISBN 978-0-615-69224-1

10 9 8 7 6 5 4 3 2 1

Dedication

My life began on July 1, 2010.
This was when I changed my vision on what I am
supposed to be doing on this earth. It was the day that I
learned that someone else depended on me for life, love
and lessons.

My story is dedicated to my Junester.
The person who gave me the purpose behind even
beginning to write this.
The person who showed me how to love beyond what I
ever knew I could.
And the person who taught me how to be the greatest
mom possible.

Mommy ADORES you Jr.!

TABLE OF CONTENTS

Intro

The minute I began thinking of the direction of this book, I was very curious to know if other moms shared my experience in becoming a new mom. The good, along with the bad, but more so, inquisitive of the bad. I thought, 'What if I gathered information from other moms to see if there are similarities in our experiences.' The things that we are often too embarrassed to say to someone else, or even feel by ourselves.

One of my best friends (who had the initial vision of this book), would call me often with concerns of how overwhelmed she felt at times and would feel relieved once I told her that I shared her same story. If it was not the exact experience, it was **very** close.

After this happened a couple of times, she came up with the idea of sharing our stories in a book to show other moms how *normal* each feeling and emotion is that we see. In doing so, we compiled a survey of questions based on circumstances/ instances that we experienced. We asked 50 moms, ages 20-35 to share their stories with us. While my friend could not continue on with the book, after reading the responses to the survey, I knew I had to push on! The responses were too great to pass up! The stories were awesome!

And now I give you: A real mom's guide to being a real mom. ☺

The Survey (My Answers)

[I conducted this survey about a whole year prior to finishing the book, however I still agree with my answers.]

1. How many children do you have? What are their ages?

    1 boy; 15months.

2. How old were you when you had your first child?

    24 years old.

3. What was your initial reaction when you discovered you were pregnant?

    I was scared! Even more nauseous than I was before knowing what was causing me to become nauseous!

4. How many months/ weeks were you when you found out you were pregnant?

    I was thirteen weeks on the dot! Three months!

5. What were you thoughts about motherhood before giving birth? (i.e. didn't want any children, believed all mothers should be married, believed teen mothers couldn't be good mothers, being a mom is 100% easy, etc.)

    I always saw myself in my mid to upper 30's having children! I wanted to be married and established in both home and career. After babysitting my nieces often, I also thought being a mom was a piece of cake!

6. What are your thoughts about motherhood now that you are a mother?

While I love my son, being a mom is hard work! People definitely aren't lying when they say that! However, I strive to be the best mother I can possibly be despite the hard times!

7. What is the meaning of a "Mother" in your culture? Do you believe you represent it well?

To me, a mother is a provider in all ways! Mothers hold so much value in life and take on so many roles without complaining. I make every effort to represent my vision of a "mother" and the value it encompasses.

8. What was your FIRST reaction of holding your child for the very first time?

I had a C-section and was still drugged up the first time I held Jr.! I remember feeling like, "WOW! I'm really holding him!" It was kind of a surreal moment!

9. After giving birth, has any of the following changed? If so, how?

(List both good and bad effects!) a. Body Image b. Sex Life c. Social Life

a. Just like most moms (who aren't blessed to bounce right back into shape or undergo liposuction!) I have the stomach problem! I probably always will--

that's just the effect of your skin stretching during pregnancy, or the results of eating too much during pregnancy. Mine was definitely the perfect mix of the two.

b. See letter "A." My body image issues have greatly impacted this! But I'm working on it! It's also hard when we both work such long days, get home and feed Jr., by then we're both exhausted and fall into deep somber!

c. HA! I barely have a social life! I go out with friends about three times a month, and that may even be an exaggeration! I do speak with them often on the telephone, but I just never seem to have much time to hang out, and when I do find time, I'm tired and much rather be laying in bed!

10. What are your biggest fears of being a mother today?

My biggest fear is not being able to protect my son at all times. This actually worries me quite often! I want to be *Super Mom* and guard him from all dangers in this crazy world. Another fear that I have is not being a *perfect* mother.

11. What is one thing you've discovered, after being a mom that no one 'warned' or mentioned before to you?

Nobody warned me that babies still don't sleep through the night after turning one year old! I'm actually upset behind this (I joke!)! My son still wakes up throughout the night, sometimes every three hours!

12. What is something you've learned from your child that affects how you are as a mother?

His innocence has completely changed me. He has no clue what's going on and it's my job to teach him. As a result, I've become way more compassionate towards family, friends, and even strangers!

13. Name one instance where you thought you had everything together, and everything fell apart (can be as simple as packing your baby bag and forgetting a key item or a little more extreme as overspending and forgetting to budget in daycare).

At the beginning, I lost everything **all** the time! Then I would lose my mind! One time I will never forget is forgetting to pack his pacifier! And I must say that I never let that happen again! One of my biggest regrets in life!

14. How has your relationship with your partner changed? Have you become closer, or has there been added stress?

There was added stress at the very beginning because I had a C- section and wasn't able to do much. I would overreact a lot, but we're **so** much closer; the closest we've ever been!

15. Do you feel your partner adjusted well to being a parent? As quickly as you?

    My boyfriend has definitely adjusted greatly, which is the best feeling because sometimes being a mom is overwhelming. Just the pressure of being a 'good' mom is enough to overwhelm you! He did not adjust as quickly as I, however, he adjusted quickly enough! It was right on time!

16. Do you find yourself being more like your mother? If so, how? If not, why?

    Hmmmm … this is a tough one! My mom was **such** a mommy! I'm not sure if I'll ever be able to measure up to my mom, but I do notice I'm way more affectionate like she was with me and my brother!

17. Are there any special traditions that you've adapted to with your child/children? Things that you love to do or plan often?

    Me and Jr. both make the craziest faces when his favorite shows come on! I call him "Gegadoo." I'm still not sure where I got that from, but we love it!

18. Did you experience any postpartum depression? If yes, explain.

Yes! See the "My Postpartum" section.

19. What is something that your baby does to **only** you? (Kiss you a certain way, or even hit you a certain way! A special or sarcastic saying! We know kids say the wackiest things!)

    My son gives me "mmmuuahhhh" kisses! Like he really says "mmmuuahhhh" when kissing me! I love it!

20. What is a classic/ favorite thing you can always catch your child saying or doing?!

    His favorite word right now is "hewo" (hello), and he also does this classic laugh that he has down packed! It's kind of like something you would see on television, when children laugh like they are really cracking up about something! It's classic!

When I initially thought of conducting the survey, I wanted to include some of the responses with the purpose of showing a variety of answers. I wanted to show differences in experiences whether they be postpartum, social life, biggest fears etc.

All of that changed after reading the replies. I was astounded at just how similar each story was to mine! How we all shared common beliefs on how we expected our lives to be after giving birth, our realities after giving birth, how motherhood affected us and how we view motherhood as a whole.

The question/ answer that I was most intrigued with was question number 7, "What is the meaning of a "Mother" in your culture? Do you believe you represent it well?" The capitalization of "Mother" was purposeful, I wanted to emphasize the title that a mother holds and how it carries as much weight as a first name.

These particular responses stuck out so much to me because it inevitably and in some cases, unconsciously made each surveyor reflect on the relationship they shared with their mother, whether good or bad. If they had a fairly good relationship with their mother, the answer was a reflection of how their mother was throughout their childhood. If the relationship was not too good, the answer reflected all the things that their mom did not do that the surveyor wishes her mother would have done. This answer ultimately came from within.

In writing the response in that moment, it forced the surveyor to visualize all of the characteristics they were describing, and in return, challenged them to question themselves, "Am I meeting these standards?" For most people, even outside of this survey, a mother is a selfless provider, guider, protector, comforter and even a friend. Comparable to a super hero in many ways by the countless noble roles she acquires.

When I had the opportunity to answer this question, I instantly began judging myself! I literally stopped and took a break after writing my response. I had to think of

16

the type of mother I wanted to be to my son and questioned if I was achieving that. At times I know I fall short of being 100%, simply because as a mother, you want to do any and everything you can for your child. However, sometimes you just do not have the strength-- you are 'anything'd' out! It is easy to feel disappointed at any time when you place so much pressure on yourself to be this perfect being, forgetting that God never created one.

"Do you believe all mothers should be married before giving birth," which is a sub question of question number 5, was another group of answers that I found shocking! I was shocked mainly because there are so many single mothers and plenty of adults from my generation who come from broken homes. I figured that the views of marriage and childbirth changed. But they did not! Over 90% of surveyors felt that children should not come until after marriage, even if they, themselves were not married at the time that they gave birth. I am sure most unmarried moms, like me, were not even planning on children until it happened, but to read that people still had such wonderful plans of marriage was great!

My desire to be married before having children was more so based on the fact that I came from a home with both of my parents and I wanted the same for my children. Seeing a great example of a marriage of over thirty years is impeccable and is reassuring that long lasting marriages are achievable.

About 85% of the surveyed moms agreed that their biggest fear of being a mother was not being able to keep their children safe and protected at all times. I totally get it. The world we live in is oh so risky on a day by day basis. There are natural disasters, abusive family members, child care neglect, fights in school etc. We would love to have a 'mom/ child radar' created just so we will know when to fly in and save our baby; even after they are not babies anymore.

Question number 18 focused on postpartum depression. I was amazed that about 45% of the surveyors experienced postpartum depression-- this was relieving being as though I was a postpartum sufferer as well (see "My Postpartum" chapter). While there is not one particular determining factor for developing this depression, its affects are powerful. A couple of surveyors noted that they were on medication for this depression, and because of its many layers, others may not have needed anti-depressants and could have still suffered heavily. Having postpartum depression does not necessarily mean that you want to hurt or harm your baby. Other symptoms of this depression are: not wanting to be bothered with baby at certain times, fear of being left alone with baby, constantly thinking that you are not worthy enough to be a mother, becoming increasingly irritable, not being able to focus on tasks, trouble sleeping and more.

As you notice, all symptoms do not include a direct connection to baby. Postpartum depression is more so generally a depression that that kicks in post birth. While it is ordinary for moms to feel *down* within the first two weeks after pregnancy, this is considered "baby blues," instead of postpartum depression. Baby blues becomes postpartum depression when symptoms last after the first month of giving birth.

While I have not done significant research on postpartum depression, I do know my experience and what my doctor shared with me when I expressed my concerns to her.

In magazines, on television, and in movies, "bad times" in motherhood are often tabooed. It is rarely discussed in detail the sometimes *overly* stressful moments. Society holds us to believe that moms are perfect; that moms can handle anything that heads their way … motherhood is made to look so easy.

I have always had the type of relationship with close friends where if they ever wanted to know anything about anything or needed advice about anything, they could come to me and I would always tell the honest truth. However, when it came to questions about my new role as a new mom, I often fabricated. I was so embarrassed of my rough times. I was ashamed of the moments that I felt defeated and I would always leave that part out and made it seem that becoming a mom was a breeze.

I was not too ashamed of my feelings after a while, and in that time I began sharing with friends who were pregnant and even friends who already had children the "**complete**" experience as I like to call it. This way, others would feel comfortable in sharing their stories and eventually feel relieved that their rough patches were not in vain.

The truth is, as mothers, we all have our bumpy moments and rough patches. We have times that we are confused and think, "I do not know if I'm doing this right," times that we feel defeated and times where we just want to cry for help. We are NOT bad moms for feeling these things, in fact if you didn't have these feelings; I think that would be a bit abnormal!

We are all great mothers, learning how to be even better mothers, so that in turn our children will be a reflection of our greatness!

My Preggo Story!
[Learning That I Was Pregnant]

I found out I was pregnant on December 23, 2009 (Merry Christmas!). But the way I found out is what is hilarious (now!).

In the fall of that same year, I attended one of my friend's birthday parties; this was some time around October 15, 2009. After the party was over, we all walked to the parking garage where I began to feel really sick. Luckily one of my best friends drove that night, but not so lucky for her, she wound up having to pull over on the interstate at about 2:00 am so that I could vomit. How disgusting! This was extremely rare for me; I never threw up, ever. I convinced myself that it was because I had too much liquor that night, which was questionable since I never over indulge on alcohol, but it was the only way I could make sense of it.

My birthday was a week later, on October 21. I had a party at home and it was so much fun! I had my family and friends all together, and I always love those times! After the party was over and everyone went home, I threw up once more! I of course thought it was too much liquor again, but this time it stuck out in my mind because I knew I never go overboard when I drink. Throwing up this time was a bit peculiar.

November came around and it's Thanksgiving season. By this time I cannot stand the taste **or** smell of alcohol. I never even knew this was a symptom of pregnancy so I completely persuaded myself that I had developed a resistance to alcohol (I am so dramatic!).

I started voicing my concerns to one of my best friend's whose parents are pastors. I asked her to ask her mother if being nauseous all the time was God's way of punishing me for eating too much! And I was ever so serious. I really thought I was being punished for being a glutton; again-pregnancy never once crossed my mind. She tried to convince me that was not it, but I didn't believe her because I started feeling sick all of a sudden **every** time I ate.

My boyfriend and I planned a wonderful trip to Las Vegas for his birthday on December 11. By this time I was soooo nauseated. The entire week leading up to the trip I felt awful. I constantly felt like I had to throw up, but nothing would ever come out when I would try. I remember using the bathroom frequently on the airplane on the way to Las Vegas. I credited this to my anxiety of being on an airplane because I had the biggest fear of flying at the time. I of course did not know that frequent urination was another symptom!

One night in Vegas, I could not take hanging out anymore, I was exhausted. I stayed in the hotel room, begged my boyfriend to go enjoy himself, and explained that I did not mind staying behind at all. I felt so bad for leaving him alone on his birthday trip, but I just could not bring myself to hanging out anymore.

Another night, we went out to eat and I promised him that I would taste a drink that contained alcohol, since I had not had any the entire trip. I was hesitant, but stated I did not want anything too strong because of what had been going on with my body. I had a tiny sip and wound up giving him the entire drink-- I hated the taste! He teased me while we were there for being such a party pooper, with us both not knowing the true reason why.

Rewind! Around the middle of October I yearned for Totinos frozen pizzas! I **had** to have them daily, my stomach practically demanded them. I started thinking that maybe my over consumption of the pizzas was the culprit behind my stomach beginning to act so weird. To add to the mystery, I also had a cycle around this same time, it was spotty, but because my cycle was always irregular, I did not even pay attention to that sign.

OK, fast forward! When we returned home from Las Vegas, I was still complaining about being sick. My dad, being the "doctor" that he is, made me drink some laxative tea because we started to think I was constipated. I had major heartburn from time to time and I told my dad that as well. He gave me his doctor's telephone number. I called the next day to schedule an appointment and to this day I clearly remember the receptionist saying, "Do you

23

think you are you pregnant? Because we can't give you an x-ray if you are."

My response was, "Oh no! There's no way that's possible." For so long my mother and I thought it was impossible for me to conceive because I had always problems with my cycle.

I secretly kept pregnancy tests by the box in the cabinet under my bathroom sink, simply because my cycle was so irregular and I did not ever want to chance anything happening. I stopped taking the tests after a while because they would always come back negative and I didn't want to continue being wasteful.

For some reason, one particular day, I felt compelled to take the one last test that I had left. I was getting ready to take a shower so I turned on the water, prepared the test (if you know what I mean!) and placed it face down on the bathroom sink. The next moment was one I will always remember!

I was so nonchalant with the test; I just **knew** it would be negative! I put my right leg up ready to step into the shower. I glanced over at the sink where the test was to turn it over and peek at the results, expecting that I wasted my time yet again. Except this time, I saw the "+" sign!

I GASPED so hard for air, one would have thought I was really having trouble breathing. I turned off the shower, threw on some clothes and walked out the house. I immediately called my best friend crying not knowing what emotion I should have at the moment.

My boyfriend was out with friends and I did not want to ruin his night without knowing for certain. My best friend instructed me, "Go to the store and buy another test to be sure." I did as I was told; I went to the store and purchased forty dollars worth of pregnancy tests. I purchased every brand possible so that there was no room for error! Meanwhile, I called my boyfriend to let him know what was going on. There was so much noise in the background and I did not want him to say anything out loud so I emphasized for him to not say or do anything obvious.

I returned home, took each test one by one and the last test said, "Shonda, you're pregnant." That is what I read in my mind! I called my boyfriend to give him an update; neither of us had any idea what to do. I had just lost my aunt to cancer in August so aborting my child was not an option at the time, but what were we going to do? Although we had been dating for a little over two and a half years by this time, we were both still young, we were both still not where we wanted to be in life, and we were both just starting to live life! WHAT WERE WE GOING TO DO?!

What and how would I tell my parents? Because this was around Christmas time, we had lots of wrapping paper, gift bags and tissue paper. My mom and dad **longed** for grandkids, so while my parents had no clue I was even

25

having sex, I knew they would not be too, *too* disappointed with the news.

I decided to wrap **all** of my pregnancy tests up in tissue paper and put them inside a gift bag. My dad worked on Christmas morning so it was perfect-- my mom was alone and I could tell them each separately. I woke up, paced around my room for a little, thinking about how or when I would actually give my mom the bag. I would walk out of my room and then back into my room, out of my room again and then down the hall. I was doing any and everything to keep from going into my parent's room where my mother was.

I finally took a deep breath and headed in. I handed her the bag.

She said, "Noooo, let's wait to open gifts when everyone is together!"

I said, "No mom, you may want to open this first."

She said, "Why I'm not going to like it?"

I said, "Ma, just open it."

She opened it and said, "There's nothing in here Shonda."

I said, "Ma, open the tissue paper."

She saw the tests, her mouth dropped; she fell to her seat in typical dramatic Linda fashion and held her heart! The very **first** thing she said was, "But you're not married."

I thought to myself, 'WHAT MOM!! I'm handing you my quarter life crisis and all you're worried about is marriage!?'

I sat on the floor and she asked, "Did you tell your dad?"

I said, "Nope, you're the first one to know" and we just sat there for a few minutes. I guess she needed time to take it in, and I just needed time, period.

My dad finally came home from work. We always have Christmas dinner before opening our Christmas gifts, so I was just waiting for my dad to take his shower and come downstairs to eat dinner. He took what seemed like **forever** to finally come downstairs.

When dinner was over, we began opening gifts. My brother handed my *secret bag* to my dad, unaware of what was inside. I screamed, "NO! That's last!"

Gift by gift by gift we opened away and it was finally my *secret bag's* turn. I handed the bag to my dad; he opened it and said, "What's this??"

My brother said very confused, "Huh? Oh, wait, dad, those are pregnancy tests. You're pregnant? I thought you were a virgin?"

27

Meanwhile, my dad is still fumbling with the sticks, even after my brother revealed what they were. After five minutes, my brother finally said directly to him, "Dad those are pregnancy tests!"

Dad says, "Ohhhh, that's what these are?! Congratulations Shonda!"

I thought to myself again, 'Huhhhh??!'

I was quite baffled! I never would have thought that all my dad would say was "Congratulations." Maybe it just did not sink in yet.

He then said, "So that's why you've been so sick!" We laughed for a little while, I then made my brother promise to not tell the world just yet and we started watching television like nothing happened. So that part-- the part that I thought would be the hardest, was over and was actually the easiest!

My mom pressed me out about going to the doctor once I mentioned to her that my last cycle was in October (again, by now it was December). Even though she knew this was not *too* weird for me considering how my irregular my cycle was, she still insisted for me to call ASAP. My mom wound up calling the doctor for me to schedule my appointment because I am very much so a procrastinator when it comes to making doctor appointments! When my mother called, the receptionist scheduled a rush appointment as soon as she caught wind of my last cycle date. I did not even know this was such a big deal at the time; I never even kept track of my cycle days since they were so 'here and there.'

The day came for my first doctor appointment. I arrived at the doctor's office and was instructed to go to the back where the sonogram rooms were after I signed in. I was about to have my very first sonogram! The sonogram technician used the transvaginal sonogram, being my first appointment, and we all assumed it would be difficult to find baby. However, as **soon** as she stuck in the probe-- we saw him, there was no need to search because he was right there! And he was FULLY formed!

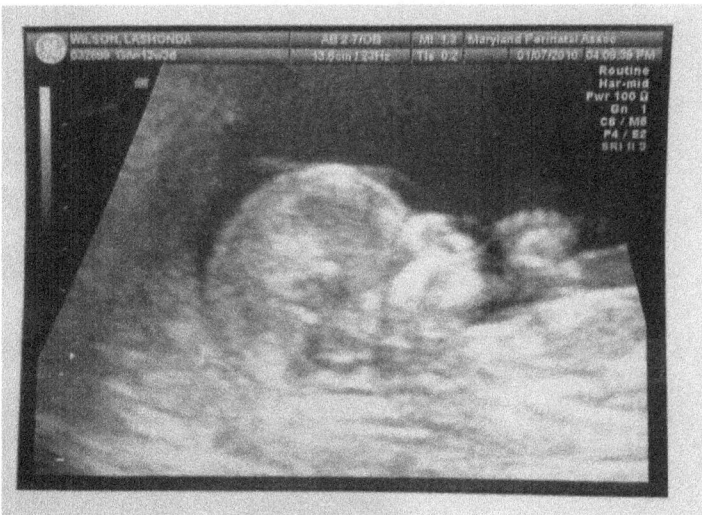

(First sonogram!)

The sonogram technician said in an astonished tone, "Oh my goodness! You're exactly 13 weeks-- 3months today; you did not know you were pregnant?!"

The truth was, although I had clues, I had no clue! She added, "Wow, the next time you come in, you can find out what you're having! People wait so long for this and you get to find out immediately!" She was so excited and I was still in shock.

Ironically, my boyfriend was shopping for a new car for about two months by this time. Whenever he would look at a two door, I would say, "I don't know why you're looking at that! You're about to start a family." Unaware that I was already pregnant! I was teasing at him because we were rarely using contraceptives at that time.

After Discovering

[During Pregnancy]

I suffered with morning sickness from about two months (back when I had no clue what was going on), and it lasted until I was six months pregnant, literally until I entered my final trimester. I remember constantly asking my mother if I would ever have a "normal" day. She would reassure me that it would get better, but month by month I would still feel horrible. I lost about thirteen pounds by the time I was five months because I could barely eat-- my body would reject everything. I began to worry. I voiced my concerns often with my doctor and she would promise me that both Jr. and I were okay.

I never threw up anything, but had the constant feeling of wanting to vomit. Food never sat well on my stomach and I was always beyond exhausted. While the latter is not unusual, being drained for about 90% of the day was dreadful. There was seldom a time where my stomach was okay, and by okay, I mean a time where I did not feel like I needed to run to the bathroom. I absolutely hated feeling this way.

I was always a heavy eater, so to me, my appetite did not change much, but the way different foods affected my body changed. By seven months, I gathered so much fluid in my legs from eating salty foods that the pain became unbearable. At one point, just lifting my leg would almost bring me to tears. I went into labor at thirty six weeks and I had gained fifty five pounds by then. And do remember, I lost weight until the end of my fifth month, so this weight gain came only from my last trimester (I was literally gaining ten pounds per week during my eight month). Scary!

My cravings: Tostinos pizzas (found in your local grocer's freezer!), baked cookies from either Subway or McDonalds, popsicles, and my **ultimate** favorite was birthday cake! One day I had a random craving for ranch dressing from a restaurant called Longhorn Steakhouse and another random day, a salad from Golden Corral buffet. The craving for Golden Corral was actually so strange to me because I am not the biggest fan of buffets.

<u>In typical preggo fashion, I threw a conniption when I did not get the food I wanted!</u> I typically ate whatever I had a craving for rather quickly because I always kept my favorites near. But one particular day, my boyfriend called to let me know that he was on the way to the house and asked if I wanted anything to eat. I said, "Pleaseeee bring me a cookie from McDonalds!!" I was so excited, but as time passed, I grew angry. My neighborhood McDonalds **always** had a long line. It was always crowded, so I was not too surprised that it took him so long, I was just upset because I wanted my cookies.

He finally arrived with bags of food in tow, but told me the most heart breaking news-- they ran out of cookies! But the next part broke my heart even more! What does he bring me for a substitute?! CHICKEN NUGGETS!! I was beyond boiling! I wondered why he didn't just bring me another snack like an apple pie instead!

I gave the silent treatment for about fifteen minutes, which I am sure he enjoyed! I later realized (about 2 whole days later!) that he brought me nuggets because that whole week I was crazy for McDonald's chicken nuggets and he was really just trying to be a great boyfriend!

Naming Baby

Giving my son a great name was something that was very important to me. A name carries so much weight in one's life, that I did not want a name that was too outlandish. I had to keep in mind my child's future. I wanted a name that either had a great meaning, or shared commonality of my boyfriend and I's name.

Long before being a mom was even a real thought to me, I began making a list of all the boys and girls names that I liked for whenever I had kids. I would update the list often so that I could get rid of the names that I once liked, but were now awful and replace them with names that I loved. I would update this list annually.

The time came **way** sooner than I expected and once my boyfriend and I finally accepted we were having a baby, I cracked out the journal in which I kept the names and shared all the names with him.

I **always** wanted my first son to be a Jr. however, my boyfriend wanted to be creative and come up with a name of our own. We could not agree on anything (our top names were Lance and Christian [although I loved the name Kyler!]). After a couple of weeks, he finally gave in and agreed on Jr.! We would have a Devin Jr.! I was so excited!

We started thinking of nicknames instantly! Strangely enough, I call him "Do da do and La La Lo," I have **no** idea where this came from, but I guess that is a part of being a mom!

Jr.'s Birthday!

[The Day He Was Born]

I so remember this day like it was yesterday! I am sure all moms do.

Wednesday, July 1, 2010 I woke up around 8:00 am, the usual since I was working from home and needed to log onto my computer to let my boss know that I was on the network. I got up from my bed and began to march in place, which was my new morning ritual. I started doing this because it hurt too bad to walk around outside because of all the fluid in my legs, yet I heard that walking helped the baby come quicker. Because I could not walk much, marching was the next best thing. It is much more force than a walk and I figured this was doing twice as much work.

I would march in place very hard and heavy in an effort to "push" Jr. down. I honestly did not think it was really working, but I guess it did have some effect. This particular morning I was marching in place, when I caught what I thought was a cramp in my stomach. I laid down for a minute thinking maybe I needed to stop marching so hard. I waited until the cramp passed, got back up and started marching again-- another cramp. I paused again, laid down until it went away, and then got back up to march some more.

The thought never crossed my mind that these were contractions because they did not hurt that bad at all, they felt more like minor cramps, even less pain than a menstrual cramp. I began marching and yet again-- a cramp. I started panicking and thought something must be wrong with the baby. Luckily my mom was working from home that day, so I went downstairs and said to her, "Mom, something is wrong."

I am guessing that labor was written all over my face because she jumped up and said, "You think you're in labor?!" She was soooo excited because that day, July 1, was her birthday as well.

I said, "No, I just keep getting cramps."

Mom replied, "You think its contractions?!" I started to have an attitude because she kept asking me labor questions and I did not think that I was in labor. I thought she was just joyful because she wanted Jr. born on her birthday.

After I clinched on to the couch a couple of times, she asked, "You want me to call the doctor?! Do you want me to call Devin?!"

I said angrily, "NO! I'm not in labor!"

I heard plenty stories of first time mothers who thought they were having contractions and got to the hospital only to be sent home. I did not want that to be me so I didn't want to overreact or assume.

After a couple of minutes, my mother called the doctor's office (against my will I might add!) and told them everything that was going on. By this time I was in the bathroom thinking I had to take a poo (TMI? I know, but that is a sign of labor!), and I heard the nurse scream, "NO! TELL HER DO NOT TRY TO USE THE BATHROOM!" So I stopped. By now I was in so much pain that I started freaking out.

My mother called my grandmother and told her to come over to ride with us because we were headed to the hospital. My mother then called my boyfriend and finally my dad and informed them as well.

The ride to the hospital was pure torture. I felt every bump, every turn, every pothole, every time my mom would push the brake. I felt every little thing.

We arrived at my doctor's office and to my luck, there was some construction being done to the parking garage and there was a wait to park the car. My mom asked me if I just wanted to walk to the entrance of the building since it was not too far, and I said yes. In my head I was still thinking, the more walking I do, the quicker the baby will come.

I blocked out everything and everyone around me and focused on getting to the entrance. I am sure people were staring at me, which is something I hate, but I honestly could not even see the people around me. I was in so much pain and grew so antsy, I just wanted to get inside and see what was going on. I was still in denial that I was in labor.

I finally got inside of the doctor's office, and guess what? There was yet another **wait**! This never happened, ever! My doctor had just left for her vacation (in which she made me promise that I would not go into delivery while she was gone), and I had to wait for the doctor in her place to get a free room because all the rooms were occupied for what seemed like **forever**. My doctor's nurse was still there and while she tried to comfort me, nothing was working.

The time came for me to go to the back and meet with the doctor, or so I thought. However, there was **still** no room available. I sat in a chair, rocked back and forth, and with every contraction I would just hold my head.

FINALLY A ROOM! The doctor was finally free! I was assigned an examining room to see what was going on with me and baby. By now, everyone in the office had time to figure out I was in labor; that is, everyone except me! I laid on the bed and the doctor began checking to see if I was dilated. This was the **worst** pain I had ever felt in my life because he checked for dilation as soon as a contraction came. This meant that he was pushing pressure upward, while baby was pushing downward.

The doctor said that I was <u>FIVE CENTIMETERS</u> dilated! <u>WHAT?! HUH?! I was really in labor?!</u> I could not believe it, but I did not have time for it to sink in. I was sent straight over to the hospital, which was connected to the doctor's office. The doctor asked me if I wanted a wheelchair and I responded, "No, I'll walk." I was still thinking that I had to get Jr. to drop down; I didn't realize that I was already so far along.

By the time I started walking over to the hospital, I was really feeling the contractions. I arrived to the delivery suites and fortunately my doctor called over and there was a room waiting for me.

To my surprise, my dad was already there! My boyfriend arrived as soon as I was situated in the delivery room. My brother showed up shortly after, and then my boyfriend's parents. Next was my aunt, then my cousin, then my other cousin, then … well you get it! There were so many people at the hospital to support Jr.'s arrival that nurses thought that my boyfriend and I were a celebrity couple. It did not all register at that moment. I was completely focused on delivering baby.

Thank God, I was able to get the epidural shortly after arriving to labor and delivery since I was so far dilated. The anesthesiologist came and administered the epidural; I was relaxed from that moment on. I even forgot what I was there for (only for a split second!). I texted my close friends to let them know that it was time. Some of them thought that I was joking because I was texting them while I was in labor, but I explained to them the power of the epidural!

Because Jr. was weighing in so large at each checkup and I was gaining weight so quickly, the doctors were expecting a nine pound or heavier baby. The doctor acting on my doctor's behalf kept pushing for a C-section because of those very notes and although I did not want one, I finally just decided to go along with it.

I was administered more than usual amounts of numbing medicine to prepare me for the C-section. I have always been able to withstand a high level of pain, so it seemed like it just was not kicking in. The anesthesiologists were so taken back. Each time they would test my skin in preparation, they would ask shockingly, "You can still feel this???"

I eventually got to the point where I told them, "Yes, but it's okay, just go ahead so I can get it over with."

They practically screamed, "NO! We'll wait!"

The meds were numbing my brain instead of my body it seemed!

It finally happened! My boyfriend said to me so excited, "LOOK, LOOK, HE'S OUT!" I of course couldn't, but he was so thrilled!

The nurse asked me, "Do you want to hold him?"

I replied, "No."

She asked again ever so puzzled, "You don't??" I was so out of it, all I wanted to do at this point was sleep.

After a couple of hours I was finally able to see everyone who came to the hospital for support and when I did, it looked like a family reunion. I felt so much love! It was amazing! That was the best part for me at that moment.

My Postpartum

[This is only my story. Not every mother will share the same experience with this depression. Some may not experience this depression at all. This was not written to frighten anyone, but more so to help others who have experienced already, and to help those who may.]

If only I knew there were so many mothers like me while I was going through this! Although my doctor did tell me how common postpartum depression was, it was still hard for me to believe that other mothers felt what I was feeling about being a mom. There were no good thoughts-- my only connection to Jr. was that I was his mother and with that, I knew that I was responsible for taking care of him. Sadly, there were days where I did not even want to look at him, moments where I felt no compassion in his tears and hours where I dreaded this new role I was given.

My story is a tad different from other postpartum sufferers. I have no raging stories of how I wanted to harm myself or my baby, which is why I never thought I was suffering from this depression. My issues were normal depression issues, but because I did not have **any** problems with depression prior to having Jr., this is what made it **post**partum depression. I would only talk about some of the bad times with my boyfriend and honestly, he would have been the only one who knew I was suffering so harshly because I hid it from everyone else out of shame.

43

I never wanted people to worry about me and I did not want to be looked at as an unfit mother.

It all started the day I returned home from the hospital. Well, let me back up, one thing that sticks out in my mind as the first sign was just moments after Jr. was delivered. When the nurse asked if I wanted to hold him for the first time and I declined. As mentioned in the previous chapter, I wanted to blame this on the medicine, but perhaps that was the first sign. I really think that this was due to the fact that I had a C-section (as I found out later that this is a contributing factor to postpartum). I wanted a vaginal birth, but the doctor kept pushing towards the C- section by saying I was not dilated enough. Looking back this is very confusing because I was dilating an inch an hour, which is great. I was already seven centimeters after being in the hospital for only two hours.

Fast forward. Because I had so many visitors throughout my stay at the hospital, I never really had a moment for everything to sink in. Once I got home, reality set in. I arrived home and was told to immediately lay down in bed. I could not be on my feet too much due to the C-section, which meant I had to rely on people for literally every move I made. I **hated** this sooooo much. I am the very independent type, I like to do what I want, when I want and because of this blasted C-section, I couldn't.

There were basic things that bothered me about this. When Jr. would cry because he was hungry, I couldn't just reach over and grab him a bottle like I could while I was in the hospital. The milk was kept downstairs in the refrigerator; therefore I had to rely on someone else to get a bottle for him. So basically, when my baby cried even in my arms for something-- I couldn't do much except ask someone else to take care of it for me.

Within two weeks, I was able to get up and walk around as I was prior to having Jr. But as soon as I was able, my boyfriend had returned to work and my mother was headed out of town for work. It was just Jr. and I. Alone. For the very first time.

I was **so** petrified of the thought. Knowing that it would just be me and him all day, with no one to help was so frightening to me. There were days where I did not want to touch Jr., but this was more so fear. I became so fearful that I was not a good mother, I was fearful that I would fail him and I was beyond fearful that someone could tell that I was not meant for this new role.

There was one day in particular where Jr. cried for so long. He was laying in his bassinet and although I reached in to pick him up, it did not help much-- he continued crying. Because I did not have much alone time with Jr. or time to figure things out, I panicked! I could not handle not knowing what to do. I called my mom crying. Fortunately, my dad was off of work that day and my mother asked him to come take Jr. for a minute. This way I would have time to pull myself back together and regroup. In that

45

moment, I felt a **complete** failure-- my own father, who had not held a baby since my brother and I were babies, could handle this more than I.

How could I not know how to comfort my own child? Why would I let him cry so long? Why was it so hard for me to figure this out?

After I got myself back together, I called one of my best friends and told her how close I came to completely breaking down. She said, "Well just don't cry Shonda." I thought to myself, 'I already did, and I feel like they'll be more tears.' I didn't want to tell her this though because by this time she was already pregnant with her baby girl and I did not want to scare her.

Whenever family and friends would call to check on me, I had to play it off; I wanted to show that I was more than capable of handling everything that was going on. I did not want anyone to know how truly overwhelmed I was. I had no choice but to grin and bear it.

There was another day that sticks out in my mind. Jr. was a little over a full month old by this time. He woke from a morning nap and just cried and cried and cried. Back when my mother was home with me, she showed me a way of rocking him in the rocking chair that got him quiet in no time! I tried that method to quiet his cry. I sat down calmly, rocked him in the chair and began humming a lullaby. It didn't work, Jr. was still crying. I thought, 'Maybe he's hungry.'

I went downstairs, quickly warmed a bottle and tried feeding him, but that wasn't it. My next move was to change his diaper-- that wasn't it. I tried singing him a song-- nope. I did everything I could think of and nothing was working. I felt **so** defeated. I sat in that rocking chair and cried with him. I pleaded with him, 'Pleaseeee stop crying because I don't know what to do.'

I did not call anyone to vent this time. I just sat there, in the chair with him and cried with him until he fell asleep. While he slept, I stayed awake and continued crying my eyes out. I eventually gave in and called my mom at work and asked her, "Mom, am I a good mom?"

She replied, "Shonda, of course you're a good mom, I had moments like that too." I thought, 'You have no idea what just happened.'

It was right then when I realized I was depressed; however I still did not feel comfortable telling anyone just yet.

Time went on and about two weeks later I received a letter from my job stating I was laid off. WHAT?! I am out on maternity leave and you are laying me **off**??

Earlier that month, I was sending emails back and forth with the Human Resources department about returning to work earlier than noted on my maternity leave papers, as they advised me I could prior to taking my maternity leave. For some reason, the HR director kept prolonging my return to work. Every time we spoke, she would come up with excuses that in turn would hold off my return. I had no clue what was going on in my absence, but I soon found out when I received that letter in the mail. Upon receiving the letter, I did not tell anyone except my parents, I didn't even tell my boyfriend. I didn't want him to get stressed out and I didn't want him to worry for me.

As soon as I told my dad, he wanted me to sue the company and while I wanted to as well, the **stress** of doing so got to me.

I was literally **so** close to moving out of my parents' home and because of my job's selfish move, I couldn't. I instantly felt horrible, on top of what I was already feeling, this was the worst timing. Here I was again, not able to provide for my child. It was a quick reminder of the days that I returned home from the hospital not being able to care for Jr. how I wanted.

Being laid off was much deeper than just being laid off to me. My job had no clue how they just ended my world. They did not think about how this affected me **and** my baby, and while I wanted to sue them for every penny, I didn't have the energy.

Every day, my dad would come home from work and tell me how to file my case, but he would not really guide me.

I am sure this is because I usually have such a *go getter* attitude and like to do things on my own. But at that time, to nobody's awareness, I was somewhere else; my mind was completely zoned out.

After all, I was home all day with Jr. I was running off about three to four hours of sleep and in comes dad home from work with a laundry list of instructions. I would ask for help, but he did not know exactly what I needed help with because I really didn't know how to voice it.

As time went on, I called a couple of lawyers to see if I had a lawful case and to seek legal advice. Each time, they would tell me I had a case, but the process was just **soooo** draining. On top of everything else I was feeling at the time, I had no motivation to put this into gear.

Staying home all day, being *locked* in the house, was not fun for me at **all**. I am so not a homebody, I was always on the go, but because the weather was changing, I did not want to risk Jr. getting sick by taking him out too much. So it was just me and Jr. all day, in the house-- I am sure I was driving him up the wall way more than he was driving me!

I kept telling friends I was still on maternity leave, which was believable because I was not set to return to work until the beginning of October and it was only the beginning of September.

While friends would come to visit me often, I still longed to be out the house enjoying life. I never really had the infamous 'me time,' I heard some mothers speak of. I started feeling like my life had somehow gone down the wrong path. I had seen friends with kids who still had time for fun and I could not find the balance. To add to my fury, I would look at my boyfriend who still found time to take a breather and I would grow so angry with him. I felt it was not fair although this was an issue I had with myself.

So now, if you are keeping up, my biggest issues were:

1. Not being able to care for Jr. the way I wanted.

2. Not being able to provide for Jr. the way that I wanted.

3. Not being able to find the balance in my *new* life.

All of this, although seeming minor, took a **major** toll on me. I had never felt so low in my life! My self-esteem suffered, my self-worth suffered, and if I kept at it, my relationship would begin to suffer. What made everything worse was not being able to tell anyone how I was feeling. Fearful that I would be judged.

I finally broke my silence when I saw how bad my irrational and quite random emotions were bothering my boyfriend. We were so close that I began taking everything out on him. I would break out crying in a normal conversation and the littlest things began to hurt my feelings. Things that would have **never** bothered me before, were.

One day, I called my boyfriend at work and abruptly said, "I think I'm suffering from postpartum."

His response, "Yea, I did think that but I didn't want to say anything that would offend you." I immediately called my best girlfriend and told her the same. She told me how common it was and recommended that I call my doctor because they had methods that could help me. I called my boyfriend right back, shared the advice with him and he agreed. The next day, I scheduled an appointment to talk to my doctor.

That was probably my best move ever! My doctor made me feel **so** much better. I told her everything that was going on, how I had been feeling, and how miserable I had become. She told me that she sees **so** many cases like this and to not be alarmed or ashamed.

She prescribed me some medication and told me to let her know if or when I started feeling better or worse. She then explained to me the side effects of the medication and they scared me to death! I will admit, I never took the pills because of the side effects, but I knew that I would start getting better since I realized and accepted what was going on with me and began talking about it.

I am **so** blessed to have such an amazing and understanding partner because he would just suck it all up and work with me! I am sure there were plenty times he wanted to express his anger with me, but he didn't and I love him even more for that!

Present day, Jr. is a week shy of turning 2 years old! I do still have *not so good*, or *"Debbie downer"* moments; actually I have them quite often! I take a lot of things the wrong way, and I am still extra sensitive at times. I am needy and extra emotional some days-- just a complete whirlwind of mess! But after discussing with other moms and discovering this was completely NORMAL, I don't place too much pressure on myself!

My overall attitude now is one of **happiness**! I don't think I will ever be my old self (both physically and emotionally), and I have accepted that! I will say, present day that I am the best me I can be and I am **beyond** proud of myself! I am ecstatic that I have overcome such a serious depression. I'm still living, I'm still loving, and I'm still learning! Life is an **amazing** gift, and I can honestly say that I truly treasure literally every minute of it! **BEYOND BLESSED!**

An update on my job: I got a new one! About a full year after Jr. was born, I returned to work. The timing was perfect because I did want to spend a year home with my baby; I just hated the circumstances.

I also started my very first business! I am the very proud Owner of The Plush Salon and Studio, a full service beauty salon located in Upper Marlboro, Maryland! This has always been a dream of mine and one day I simply stepped out on faith! This entire journey has been astounding and this is only the beginning!

Currently speaking, I am not going to sue my old job anymore, although the thought does run through my mind ever so often, but I then think, they are so not worth it! What goes around comes around; I look at my blessings and forget all about them! God will handle that! And I will be waiting with popcorn to sit back and enjoy the film! ☺

Not Feeling So Mommy-ish
[Not Feeling Like A Mom Just Yet. Again, this is only my story!]

This chapter means **so** much to me, solely based on my experience entering motherhood. It took me one full year to feel the mommy/ baby attachment that I had heard most mom's feel as soon as they hold their baby for the first time. As redundantly mentioned in previous chapters, I denied holding Jr. when he first came out of the womb. I at first attributed this to me being drugged up from the medication, but as time went on, I still did not feel the, "This is **MY** baby!!!" connection that I predicted, I am sure this has something to do with my postpartum depression as well.

After discussing this *issue* with other moms, I noticed that this was seemingly more prevalent than I had assumed. Mothers do not like to reveal these feelings because they are often embarrassed or extremely guilty for having ever felt this way. I was the same way. I never bought this up to anyone, ever; not even to my boyfriend with whom I share everything. I did not feel good about what I was feeling (or was not feeling for that matter) and I didn't want to be judged.

While my "mommy instincts" did kick in, in that I was overly nurturing and wanted to take care of my baby; I still did not feel the overwhelming joy that most moms talk about on television and that I read about in parent magazines. While I wanted to be overcome with excitement, there were plenty of days where I just went with the flow.

By going with the flow, I mean I accepted my role as Jr.'s mom-- without the connection of being Jr.'s mom. I will explain even further-- I wanted to do everything I could for him, simply because that is a women's nature, but I did not in any shape or form feel like his mother, or **a** mother for that matter.

I thought that this would change after a couple months; I expected that before long I would feel like this astounding mom that I often saw at malls, when I would go out to eat at restaurants or that was often depicted in films-- but I didn't.

One thing about me is that out of **all** of my friends, both near and far, schoolmates, family members, etc., I was the last person anyone expected to become pregnant! I was so terrified at the thought of being in a relationship at the time and extremely private-- nobody even knew how serious I was with my boyfriend. And while I adored kids, I knew I was not ready for children of my own. I wanted to be much older, settled into my own home, married, and successful in my career all before I even thought of having children.

People were shocked (to say the least), when they found out I was pregnant, but not much more than me. I tricked myself into thinking that raising my son would be much like babysitting my nieces (hi Mikayla, Courtney, and newbie Amari!). I thought that parenting couldn't be too hard and I would adore him just as much, if not more than I had adored them. I babysat my nieces so often that I just knew raising my son would be a breeze. I was OVERjoyed when I had them for the weekend! They were soooooo much fun! They had so much personality and were just so innocent; I thought there is no way having a child of my own could be any different!

The one thing I neglected to realize, that probably was key, was the clear as day fact that my nieces were going back home to **their** parents after the two days they spent with me! I did not have the full responsibility or commitment of being their parent. I never even thought about the amount of work that actually went into raising a child of my own.

I remember seeing my son for the first time. He was beautiful, the cutest baby I had ever seen! … Yet it did not feel real. The moment seemed just as a moment. It did not sink in that this was **my** son. Although I knew I had a baby inside of me for thirty seven weeks, even after hearing Jr.'s cry for the first time-- I did not feel the connection. I just assumed the responsibility of being his caretaker because I **knew** that was my job.

Over time, I grew accustomed to feeling this way. I began thinking that this must be what every mother feels and maybe I just had the wrong expectation of how I should

56

feel. Even after being with my Jr. all day, rocking him to sleep each night, feeding him throughout the day, holding him while he cried, laughing and joking with him-- I still felt nothing. I not once grew concerned because again, I thought this was how it was for all moms and thought that other moms had to be faking it to others just as I.

It was not until a full month after Jr.'s first birthday that I actually **felt** that he was my son. I gave birth to this wild little fellow running through the house! I had created such a smart, witty baby who looks just like me! **THIS IS MY SON!** I became even crazier over Jr. too! I **finally** felt like I was his mother and I soooo loved it!

I started making up for lost time instantly! I didn't want to go away too long without him and if I did, I was either talking about him or looking at pictures of him the entire time I was away. I may have physically been away from Jr., but I could not have a break from him in my mind (although I did need one from time to time!).

I became glued to him, to his spirit; I felt like our lives were connected. Even though we were together so much while he was a newborn, just being around him felt different. My heart was heavy thinking about him-- in a remarkable way. I could really feel him in my heart. This was a new feeling for me and while I loved my son prior to having this revelation, I adored him even more!

I have no reasoning to the lack of connection, I am not even sure if there is one. I'm not certain if there is a time limit on feeling mommy-ish, or if there is a special cue that God sends that is like, "Snap into it already!"

For those who are lucky, it happens it an instant, while for others like me, it takes time to accept the mommy role you are blessed to take on … and that is completely okay!

My advice to those who are in the same boat as me is to **wait it out**. Before long you will feel overjoyed without even feeling guilty of your past feelings. Your unconditional love will over power your guilt. You will not even think of how you once felt as soon as this sensation encompasses you!

I actually forgot that I had ever felt this way until a new mom asked me if I 'felt attached to Jr. when I first had him.' I saw the concern in her eyes when she asked, and I wanted her to know that what she was feeling was acceptable and that she was not an awful mother for not adjusting as quickly as she thought she should.

If you too are like me, there is no rush to adapting, and quite honestly there is not much that can be done to speed up the process. I believe that as long as you are on your mommy duties and you are doing all that you can to make your baby feel loved despite how you feel inside-- the attachment will completely take over in time!

The Not SO Sexy Life
[Post Baby Sex Life]

Intimacy - did you forget what that was?! It is not hard to lose sight of romance once you bring home baby, in fact, majority of surveyors agreed that after bringing home baby, there was more of **no** intimacy than little intimacy. Most couples will concur that having an intimate, private moment is a thing of the past and extremely rare once you have children. And this is not hard to believe; just think, all of your time and energy is devoted to your new baby. You both share a new focus and dedication; it is very easy to lose sight of something that is just as equally important. Even having an on call sitter or loving mother who is willing to help with baby whenever you need does not help much, because even in those moments, the very first thing you want to do is rest.

While it becomes typical to neglect each other from time to time, it is very important to keep the "spice" post baby. Not with the purpose of making another (unless you are ready!), but to maintain a level of intimacy. *Feeling* wanted is one of the best reassurances after having a baby, knowing that your partner still finds you sexy despite your new pajama wardrobe and messy hair makes you feel as though you are the most beautiful woman alive!

About sixty percent of the surveyed women reported that they returned to their normal sex life after baby was born.

59

This number surprised me greatly! My assumption was that if women were not feeling too good of their bodies (which were the biggest 'issues' after having a baby), that they would then be too embarrassed for their partner to look at their new bodies-- let alone touch them. About fifteen percent stated that their sex life had gotten even better, while the remaining twenty five percent stated that it took them a couple of months to return to their old sexual selves.

I dug a little deeper to discover the reason of these answers:

Women who reported that it took them a bit of time to readjust to their old sex lives stated that this was mainly due the fact that new baby does not allow much time for intercourse. The other popular reason was not accepting their new body, which I like to call, "The Not Feeling So Sexy" condition. The latter was definitely my issue. I admittedly was ashamed and embarrassed of each belly roll and love handle that had developed after Jr. was born.

Women who reported going back to the same or even better sex lives stated that they had low or fair body image issues. They added that while they did have minor riffs with themselves, that they did not let it control them. I was furthermore curious to know if these particular women had returned to their same size, or similar size prior to baby, or if they simply embraced their new curves. And that was it! While most agreed that they did have some body conscious areas, they were however in love with their new proportions.

I would also like to state that some women commented on their better sex lives being relatable to feeling more of a "woman" after having baby. The overall birthing process gave them a sense of empowerment. They wanted to take control and express their love to the person who gave them such a special gift.

After having a baby, being sexy definitely comes from within. The overall *feeling* of sexy is completely in your mind. There were days where I knew I looked the exact same as the day before, but if I set in my mind that I looked nice that day, I actually felt it. Once you can find it in you to *feel* sexy when you look in the mirror, the world around you will look better as well! Your confidence will start soaring through the roof and your entire demeanor changes. You become more approachable when speaking with others. You find a way to hide your flaws in wearing the perfect outfit. You begin to actually feel good about yourself.

To keep the romance, I developed relationship rules for my boyfriend and I to follow. I initially wrote them out as pointers for myself, and then I decided to share them with him. Once he agreed we stuck to our rules monthly!

Rule 1: Designate at least thirty minutes per day to focus on each other.

Whether this was just recapping how our days went, discussing our future, or even talking about something random like a television show that reminded us of one another. We had to take out the time to talk only amongst ourselves, about ourselves.

Rule 2: Date nights/ weekends.

My boyfriend and I were always on the go before Jr. We loved spending time with each other and did practically everything together. This understandably grew hard and after having no quality time, I was fed up and decided to do something about it! I worked up a sure fire plan that would eliminate this problem. We began putting aside two nights per month for a date night. Date nights were nights where we would go to a fun restaurant, check out a movie at the theater, or even just sit at home by ourselves, eat tacos, and drink margaritas (he makes these so well!).

To take date night a bit further, we would combine the two days set aside for date night and create a date weekend. We would get a nice hotel room for the night, hang out all day and night and just enjoy each other's company.

Rule 3: Mini Getaways.

This one was rather hard to keep up with because we did not like travelling too much and leaving our son to *burden* someone else, however we knew that every once in a while, we deserved a mini break. Our annual trip was to

Virginia Beach to celebrate our anniversary. This was because this was our very first trip that we had ever taken together. Each year, the trip was super fun and because it held so much significance, we **always** made time to go.

Winning Back Your Old Self Esteem

Not feeling the greatest after having a baby is almost inevitable. Looking yourself in the mirror and feeling confident can be quite the challenge. You may not pay this too much attention the first few days after birth because you are so consumed in baby, and not to mention, during your hospital stay there is not much time to have a good look in the mirror. Once you do have this chance, you will be amazed at how much you have changed and you may grow doubtful that you will ever return to your *old self.*

You actually adapted to your stomach carrying a five plus pound fetus, and you never stopped to think of what would happen after nothing was inside.

So sad, but so true, those extra pounds turned into minor flab! It is nothing uncontrollable, but that trivial adjustment alone is enough to make you go slightly crazy and run to the nearest gym.

Speaking for myself, six out of seven days of the week I hated the way I looked! I was completely disgusted at the person facing me in the mirror. I hated putting on clothes; I even hated shopping for clothes because of the size I would read on each tag. In typical Shonda fashion (in that I am very overdramatic!), going into public became a chore for me, I absolutely hated it. I had much rather stayed inside the comfort of my home and watch television. It got to a point where I did not want my boyfriend to look at me! Even if he told me I was beautiful, I didn't believe it. I was **so** hard on myself.

Rebuilding self-confidence is what I struggled with most. I was not accepting of my flaws, and more importantly-- I did not encompass the assurance to step into the world and feel great about myself. Accepting my new rolls was something that would come later, however if I **felt** good about myself, it would show, and if I didn't, others (even complete strangers), could pick up on it.

After complaining to my boyfriend on several occasions about how I looked, I realized I was creating an undesirable space between us. He did not even notice my flaws as much as I and continuing to point them out all the time had become a complete turn off! I had to think quickly! I began making rules for myself that I had to live by! I called them, "Self Rebuilders" and for me, it was the only way to snap out of it! No more putting myself down!

My Self Rebuilders:

1. While laying in bed each morning, I would say, "Remember you are beautiful and anybody is lucky to have you." Not that I wanted '*anybody*' per se, I was completely head over heels with my boyfriend, however, I had to remind myself that to the world, I was beautiful; a lucky charm, a perfect match, and a treasure to complement any man!

2. While getting dressed, I would say out loud, "You JUST had a baby and you still look amazing!" This wasn't hard to say, but it was **very** hard to believe, however in time, I noticed that I really did not look as bad as I thought. I could have been much worse, and instead of putting myself down with every outfit I'd put on, I began embracing my new body.

3. After getting dolled up and ready to head out, I would look myself in the mirror and say, "WOW! You are a firecracker!!!" That was the icing on the cake! I forced myself to believe that I was beyond beautiful! That I could turn heads without even trying! That I was the best thing walking! Not with the purpose of thinking too highly of myself, but more so, to get me thinking of myself period!

4. Throughout the day, saying, "You are a **mother**, the greatest force on the planet!" would make me feel like a conqueror and I would forget about every negative thought of myself, and instead remember that I brought life into this world!

5. Going clothes shopping was something I used to dread! But I found a way to make it fun! The mirror and your mind are crazy forces when they are combined! In my head, I was still the size I was when I was carrying my son inside of me! I truly thought I still looked six months pregnant! And while my sizes aren't totally outrageous, my

proportions are different and I had to remember that just because my clothing sizes are larger now, it doesn't mean it's a bad thing!

My shopping secret: I would go into stores and purchase one size bigger than what I wore. When I got home to try the items on, needless to say, the clothes were too big and I needed a smaller size! It was FANTASTIC! My best idea yet!

6. Instead of fishing for compliments from my boyfriend, who probably did not know how awful I felt about myself and would 95% of the time say the wrong thing! I instead would ask close friends how I looked in certain outfits! I asked friends who I knew would be honest, but in a nice way.

   I would take pictures of myself with my cell phone and send to about two or three friends just to make sure I looked okay before stepping out! This way, even if my boyfriend didn't give me the compliment I wanted right away, I would still feel assured in what I was wearing!

Sometimes what we see isn't a true reflection of us, but more so of how we interpret ourselves! Once you are able to fully accept the new you regularly (having bad days are completely acceptable!), notice how your self-esteem, self-confidence, and even self-respect changes!

You will begin to finally love yourself again and it is the greatest, most self-rewarding feeling ever!

Woe Is Us

[** I stress that this chapter was written to express that you and your partner may have a rough patch during the adaptation period with baby. It was not written in support of unhealthy or dysfunctional relationships.]

The reason most couples appear to have it all together after having a baby is because they **want** it to look that way, but trust me when I say; each couple has their own cross to bear after bringing home a newborn.

To the outside world, my boyfriend and I were the *perfect* couple. We barely argued, we were always smiling, we appeared to be so wrapped up into each other and while this was not far from the truth-- we had a major time adjusting together after Jr. We were **so** unexpectedly stressed that some days it was close to unbearable.

I would take things out on him, he would take out things on me, and at some points, we questioned if we were still compatible. We did not know that what we were experiencing was normal and we just wanted the arguing to stop. We thought the only way to getting back to how we were before having Jr. was to take a break from each other and let things calm down. Of course love would not allow this to happen, but that is just how rough it *can* get.

Your relationship is number one after having a baby. While some have mastered this prior to having a baby, **now** everything and everyone literally takes a back seat and you start to not care who does not like it. After all, this is the person whom you are sharing the rest of your life with. This is who helped you create such a wonderful gift and all you want to do it soak it all up in as many ways possible.

I barely made time for hanging out with friends once Jr. joined me in life because if by chance I had any free time, I wanted to spend it with my boyfriend! I wanted to make sure our relationship was unbreakable and that we still shared the same bond that we had months before. I wanted to ensure that we remained solid and built on our foundation. Remaining best friends was my goal.

A great relationship was so important to me because I knew if we were happy, then that meant our baby was even happier! It meant that our baby was surrounded by our love and could see and feel our bond!

But honestly, no relationship is guaranteed sun shining rainbows and white fluffy clouds after having a baby-- even if you were the "perfect" couple. You **will** experience some true tests that can make or break your relationship, and while I hope that these tests make you two stronger, the fact is that most couples have experienced their roughest moments after bringing home baby. In most cases, this has nothing to do with their love for each other, but more so elevated stress levels.

I am a firm believer in there being no set rules or guidelines to which a relationship should follow when it comes to arguing and apologizing. My boyfriend and I found ourselves in this category more times than not after having Jr. While we hated it, the truth is, there were a great number of moments where neither of us even knew what we were upset about and because we were so stressed, it was so easy for us to take it out on each other since we are so close. We did not realize, or even understand that we both had to adjust to our new roles at our own individual speed.

Being the mommy that you are, you expect your partner to snap into parenthood at the same pace as you. You then expect them to know how to react to each situation as they arise, and even one step further, you expect them to do the impossible-- read your mind and know exactly when, how and what you need help with automatically!

In addition to not getting much sleep, baby crying at random times throughout the day, your draining work schedule, your hormones still being off balance, and you hating how you look; you neglect to think that your partner may be experiencing your exact post baby blues. While this *non recognition* may be completely unfair to daddy, it happens. Adding to this, because men typically do not voice their inner feelings, it becomes something mommy has to lookout for.

For new daddy, catering to new mommy's needs is expected. They are prepared and aware that mommy is still going to be seemingly irrational and emotional at times. In this same token, you (mommy) must recognize that no matter how big, brave and prideful daddy is, he is allowed these equal moments too.

Many couples do not discuss their relationship woes with outsiders, which I agree is **very** smart; however, because of this, many couples are not prepared for the mini battles you may face after baby. You begin to think that something is wrong with you *or* him and some couples become so overwhelmed that they begin to doubt their relationship.

There may be days where mommy does not think that daddy is doing all he can, and daddy may have days where he feels like mommy is being overbearing. Mommy may want a day off from mommy duty and daddy may have moments where he wants a time out as well.

Often times, mommy and daddy share the same viewpoints regarding one another. It becomes second nature to completely dismiss each other's feelings because both parents see themselves as the only one who is rightfully stressed. Blind sighted to the fact that both parties are entitled to their own overwhelming moments.

The key (so I have found), is to start **paying attention** to what each party (mommy and daddy) needs from each other regarding the relationship and their new role as parents. The next part (which is just a tad tricky), is to now respect what you need from one another, without taking anything personal.

By this I mean, if your partner wants to be left alone, give him a minute without thinking he wants time away from you or baby. If your partner wants to take a nap, allow so without thinking that he does not deserve one. If your partner does not want to change a diaper, cut him some slack without pointing fingers of what you have done all day. Now let me make clear that I am not saying allow your partner a free pass to the point where you have taken on majority of the responsibility; I am simply saying allow your partner the same *privileges* that you are expecting him to give you.

Another challenge and one that I have found to be most rewarding is taking out the time to pinpoint exactly what your partner is trying to convey to you **without** them saying it to you. Your partner may not want to open up when you want them to and/or they may not even know how. It is not an easy task to automatically know what your partner is feeling without them expressing these thoughts; however once you become accustomed to understanding your own feelings, it becomes easier to pick up on theirs.

Personally, I did not **understand** what I was experiencing enough in myself to be able to explain these feelings to my

73

boyfriend. I merely thought I was on the verge of going insane, however I did want to get to the root of the problem. In the end, I discovered that we both needed our own time to adjust separately. After sitting down with myself to evaluate what was going on and why, it became easier to have talks with him.

The secret to maintaining a healthy relationship is healthy disputes, even after you bring home your new addition! Do not feel shameful for having these mini riffs with your partner. Even though having a baby is one of the most enjoyable times of your life, it is not a walk in the park for either person involved. Be open to the fact that daddy is allowed to have just as many bad minutes, moments and days as you.

After all, it is a team effort and while the saying is, "A happy wife, a happy life," it is definitely the same for husband's too!

No Nannies Allowed!
[Quick Recap]

While the title of the book suggests that I have a vengeance against nannies-- that is so not the case! The ultimate purpose of my book is to share my experience of being a new mom today with those who have already experienced motherhood and those who are preparing for the big day! Hence the second part to the title, "A Real Mom's Guide to Being a Real Mom."

While nothing in life can prepare you for one of the best experiences in life, oxymoronically-- you must be prepared! We are all warned of the restless nights, we know of how loud baby's cry can grow when they are upset and we know that their first sickness will freak us out more than they. What we learn along the way is, these moments are just as precious as your baby opening their eyes for the first time and the first time they smile at you, simply because all of these moments pass ever so quickly.

Spending a great amount of bonding time with baby is important for both you and baby. Mommy and baby bonding shapes the relationship you will have with your baby. My belief is that that once baby becomes accustomed to seeing mommy's face, embraces your comfort, feels your heartbeat, and gains trust in you, that the mommy/baby bond is everlasting.

After delivery at the hospital, you have ALL the help that you would not even appreciate until you return home! You do not have a chance to get hungry because your nurse makes sure you eat often, your little one is bathed each morning, checked regularly; and then visiting family and friends take care of you and baby around the clock too!

As soon as you arrive home from the hospital, reality sets in! You are officially **Full Time Mommy**! While times get hard, you love your baby with all your heart and want to do everything you can for them. You panic when they cry, you fall asleep rubbing their back to get them to sleep, and move your quickest to get them a bottle when they are hungry-- all because you are mommy and you want to. It is an obligation where you do not even feel obligated.

You had ample time planning for this new life you are encompassing during those thirty to forty weeks of pigging out and swollen feet! And while each baby differs, as mothers we all share common stories. We all stress to ensure our babies are healthy, we want to hug and kiss them all day long, we want to dress them in the cutest outfits, we want to protect them from the universe, and of course, we want to get some rest as soon as they shut their eyes too!

It is a hard **job** being a mother, which I did not understand until I gave birth. While I was blessed with the opportunity to spend my son's first year at home with him-- I was in a sense, **still at work!** Currently, my son is over a year old and still does not sleep through the night. He ate every two hours until he was about four months old, every three hours until about five months old and then every four hours until he was about seven months old. Needless to say, I was on my toes quite often! Not to mention teething (and getting the common ear infection along with it!), Jr. being sick for the first time, and the infamous crawling stage will definitely keep you very busy!

<u>Down time? What's that?!</u> That goes right out of the window! And while you have spells where you miss having free time, you don't want to miss out on too much time away from your baby!

My parents, grandparents, and my boyfriend's parents were awesome while I was adjusting to becoming a mommy. I definitely had times where I became beyond overwhelmed! Although I watched my nieces often prior to Jr. being born, Jr. was **nothing** like them! His personality literally developed at five months (I have video footage to prove this), and he has been on a roll since!

I needed help like never before, even if it was just to take a ten minute catnap! Oh, and if I just so happened to have a full twenty four hour break, I did not know what to do with myself … besides **sleep**!

Being a full time mom, on top of working a full time job, on top of being a great spouse does have its rough moments, but it is something we willingly signed up for after checking the imaginary "yes" after discovering we were pregnant.

<u>Is there a way to balance it all?</u> Although it does not look like it at first, there is light at the end of the tunnel. You will adapt quicker than you know, and if not, you will appreciate the time it took to adapt!

Through this entire process you learn **so** much about yourself.

You learn how much patience you have.

You learn how much like your own mother you are.

You learn to become more structured, more punctual, and even more responsible.

You learn that you are a force to be reckoned with at **all** times and you dare someone to cross you or your baby.

You learn that despite how hard you have to be with baby, that they are softest place in your heart.

You learn that friends will come and go, and the ones that matter are the ones who stay around.

You learn that family is family and nothing can separate you from them, so in turn you love them and appreciate them even more.

You learn how to get in your groove. You set a schedule that you stick to without even thinking about it.

You learn to make the most out of your weekends, even if it is only catching up with rest.

You learn to appreciate your parents in a different way. You totally get why they did the things that they did and what they went through raising you.

You learn your true purpose and begin reveling in it. You think back to your dreams as a child and start taking the steps to live them just so you can show your children that it can be done.

You learn and you conquer. You live and you love harder. You play and work smarter. You guide and provide. You gain wisdom and knowledge along the way. You appreciate both the good and bad of your journey!

While I have not learned the secret to balancing it **all**, I **have** learned how to create a balance in every aspect of my life and once you learn to do this, everything seems to come together perfectly.

You are a real mom doing real mom things. Having a real mom experience. Living a real mom life. And despite the rocky road, there is nothing you would do to change it!

Have fun new moms! Take time to reflect old moms! We made it through the most life changing experience that we will ever encounter!

We are all super moms in our own way. From whatever we went through to make it-- relish in the fact that we did!

I encourage you all to share your stories! Do not be ashamed of your low moments, instead love and appreciate them along with your happiest because they too made you the mommy that you are today!

Rock on moms and remember NO NANNIES ALLOWED!
… I kid ☺

THE GUIDE

1. **Bond with baby!** Your nurse will stress how important the first few days are for bonding with your newborn. Whether this is holding baby close so they can listen to your heartbeat, singing a lullaby so they can hear your voice, or even making sure you are the first face they see each time they open their eyes.

   Because I had a C-section to deliver Jr., it was difficult for me to go back and forth to his bassinet in the hospital. I would always have my boyfriend wake up, hand me Jr., and I would then let him go back to sleep. I wanted that special time to hold Jr. close and say little phrases in the same tone I used while he was inside of my belly. I also knew during the day, I would have many visitors, so the perfect time for my bonding was at night. After a long day, any time after 10:00 pm my boyfriend was exhausted. I would let him know that it was okay to go to sleep so that I could *cheat* extra alone time in!

2. **Adapt to your new sleeping schedule (or lack thereof!)** Mommy's (and even non-mommy's), know how exhausting life is with a newborn. The saying, "You sleep, when your baby sleeps,"

becomes your new words to live by! Whether your newborn sleeps every five hours, or every two hours, you must learn to sleep when they do. Your rest is very important; you cannot function properly without sleep.

The good thing about newborns sleeping patterns are, they only wake to eat and typically go right back to sleep within a short amount of time. Daytime with baby is generally easier than nighttime simply because our bodies are naturally more responsive when the sun is up. Take **plenty** of naps throughout the day; squeeze in twenty minutes if that is all you have. When family and friends come over, do not be afraid to ask them to watch your little one while you sleep. Without proper rest you become irritable, unhappy, frustrated and in some cases delusional.

There are a couple of things you can do throughout the day that will help you function on little rest.

a. Have a protein shake. Protein shakes have the nutrients needed for an energy boost and are also a great idea because they double as a meal supplement as well in the moments that you do not have enough time to make yourself a meal.

b. Take a hike! Well, not literally but a quick stroll around the block with your newborn in their stroller gets both your body and blood flowing which in turn provides energy. This also doubles as a quick workout!

c. Listen to *fun* music! Fun music is music that makes you want to sing and dance along. It is great for keeping your spirits up and your body busy. You will not have much time to focus on sleep if you are listening to your favorite Beyonce tune!

While these tips will never replace a full nights rest-- they will definitely help in the moments where you **need** energy.

3. **It is okay to *hate* your body!** This is one of the biggest issues after having a baby, and can actually linger into later years.

   Honestly, after giving birth, weight will be an issue, it does not matter who you are. Some people are blessed to go right back to their old size, while others have to work out a bit. Some lose more weight than intended, and some do not lose any weight until a couple of years later. It is absolutely fine to look like you just had a baby when you just had a baby. Embrace it!

4. **It is okay to cry!** Let it out! You are overwhelmed, you are not feeling yourself, and you just need a

breather! Baby can take so much out of you and your emotions are everywhere. Breaking down or, 'having a moment' is completely acceptable. Nobody understands what you are going through except **you**! If crying will help you deal with your stress and anxiety, again-- let it out.

5. **It is okay to be needy!** Some days you really feel like crap! All you want to hear from your partner is, "Baby you are doing a wonderful job," or, "You are so beautiful," and it would make your day! Men do not get this as quickly as we do, so if you feel like you NEED to hear a compliment-- it is okay to seek one from your partner.

   This was very hard for me to adjust to because before having Jr., I was very confident. To actually *need* to hear my boyfriend say how much he loved me or how much he thought I was attractive was pretty major. I was in a complete vulnerable state, compared to my head strong state before. In time, I did not care how needy I looked, if I needed to get a pat on the back from time to time, I learned to simply ask for it because my boyfriend would not naturally know each time I needed to hear him say something nice.

6. **Overcome "mommy instincts" to let daddy enjoy his experience too!** If you are like me, you like to have things your way, you are very organized, and

you panic when you seem to not have control. You trust your "mom instincts" on practically everything and you somehow know what each cry is that your baby belts out, you know when your baby wants to be held, you know when your baby is about to wake from sleep, and you know when your baby wants nothing at all! You know, you know, and you know! And because you know your baby, it sometimes makes it difficult for daddy to know as well! Allow daddy an opportunity also! After all, without daddy there would be no baby!

It is not the easiest to leave baby with daddy at first. You want to make sure everything is smooth sailing. But believe it or not, daddy loves baby as much as you and would not want to harm baby any more than you would. After you help daddy begin to figure things out, take a step back!

Wanting to be the best parent is awesome! My boyfriend and I used to have playful competitions surrounding this! It only made us work harder to be great parents together! We wanted a strong relationship with our son and wanted him to know that both of us were here for him equally. While my boyfriend is **way** more playful than I am with Jr., Jr. knows that when he wants a kiss for his 'boo boo' or a hug after he gets out of the bath, that I am the go to, however when it is time for playing "dunk" (catch!), learning to ride his bike, or anything that involves the outdoors, that daddy is his guy!

This is something we started when Jr. was still a wee baby! We wanted him to know and understand our very different, yet significant roles!

7. **It is okay to say <u>no</u>!** Expect **every** aspect of your life to change! After all, your new focus will be your new baby! The little chances that you get to take a break; you will want to spend resting. Do not feel guilty or afraid to tell people you do not want to do something or go somewhere. Do not feel obligated to anything or anyone … Friends and family understand!

8. **It is okay to *doubt* yourself.** While you are carrying baby inside of you, you have no idea the experience you will face once they enter the world. No niece or nephew can prepare you for your life changing experience! There may be times where you think that you do not measure up to the image of being a great mother, when the reality is-- only a great mother would think this! That extra push from within is really all you need to be the best mother that you can be.

My battle with motherhood was feeling like I could not measure up to my mother. Growing up my mother did it ALL! She was the perfect example of housewife meets hard worker. My mom cooked **every** evening (Friday's and Saturday's were our take out nights), cleaned the **entire** house weekly, washed and ironed **all** of our clothes **every** Saturday morning! She helped us with our homework daily, attended PTA meetings, and ensured she had relationships with **each** of our teachers every year (until we reached high school and forced her to stop!). She was the ultimate wonder woman in my eyes!

Because my mom did so much, my brother and I were completely spoiled! I did not do laundry until I went away to college; I barely cooked, barely washed dishes, etc. After I had Jr. there were days where I thought, 'I can't do this, I'm not a mom.' I had to realize, "I'm not **my** mom, but I *can* be in time." And that worked greatly for me!

9. **Patience IS key!** You have a new pressure in your life and learning how to cope can be incredibly draining. Give yourself time to adapt, there is no rush. Your love for your little one is not compromised while allowing yourself time for patience.

   While I was pregnant with Jr., everyone (literally everyone), would say, "You are going to realize how much patience you have once you become a mother." And whether this revolution be good or bad, you in turn will realize exactly how much you **need**!

My patience is as thin as a piece of notebook paper. I like to have things done when want to have them done, I like things in a specific order, and I do not like waiting on others to complete tasks. One thing I discovered about my patience however, is when it comes to my son, all of that is out of the window. Granted, I do still have my antsy moments, but that's common.

10. **You are allowed** *bad* **days!** Just as you have bad days at work, you may also have bad days in parenting. Being a mommy is a fulltime job! There may be days that you are completely beat and feel defeated. Especially at the very beginning; feeling 'not so great' at times is expected! Take a break, mope around, do whatever you have to do to carry out that moment! You are a mother, **not** mother Theresa, and nobody expects you to be.

11. **Be sure to schedule "ME" time!** Every second counts now! After a long day, and an even longer night of caring for your little one, you will definitely forget about yourself from time to time! Scheduling time for yourself is a must! Even if it is only ten minutes out of the day, be sure to devote those ten minutes to you and you only!

12. **Be sure to schedule couple time!** Because mommy and daddy are embracing their new roles as parents, it becomes easy to neglect their roles as partners; which is how baby got here to begin with! Do not lose the romance or significance of what made your relationship special! Intimacy, communication, and most of all feeling loved and wanted are all so very essential during this time. Talk to your partner often about how you feel, about what you want from each other, and always share how much you love one another!

    Put aside date nights that are reserved for the two of you! If you cannot go out, after putting baby to sleep, play a fun game together, cozy up and watch a movie, anything to make your quality time enjoyable!

13. **Treat yourself!** This was one of my hardest things to do in the months after giving birth! I was so consumed in buying diapers and baby clothes that I began neglecting myself! It got so bad that at one point, I didn't even have anything decent to wear to go purchase the diapers and baby clothes! When it came time to go shopping for myself, I would somehow wind up inside of a baby store and spend away on Jr.!

    It is imperative to maintain yourself as you were before baby, or take it a step further, look even better! Purchase clothing items that you've always wanted. Items that will flatter your new shape and curves!

14. **Embrace the NEW you!** Are you more like your mother? Are you overly sensitive? More driven? A homebody?

    Well, whatever the case may be, this is the new you! Love it! Soak it all up! There is nothing upsetting about that! Having a baby only brings out the best in you!

    After having Jr., I've become way more confident in pursuing my dreams! I have the drive to do everything that comes to mind just to make him proud! I long for the day that he says, "My mom rocks!" I now have the push and desire to constantly think of my next move, and I believe that as mothers, we all do! We want to do everything that we can to make our children proud.

    Do not be afraid to face your fears and live the thoughts that are plaguing your mind! Love **who** you have become and love **what** you have become. Rejoice in the new you!

15. **Balancing Act.** You are not a superhero and no one expects you to be. You have to take time to figure out who and what is most important in your new

life now and prioritize accordingly. You will not be able to see everyone or do everything that you used to, it is nearly impossible.

However, keep up the good work! Don't be too hard on yourself. In due time, it all will fall into place and you will learn to be mommy, wife, professional, chef, playmate, daughter, best friend, and whatever else you deem for yourself! You **can** do it all and more!

Tip: I find it easy to get things done by setting daily goals for myself. I purchased an 'in depth' planner and literally write down everything so I do not forget a thing, from tasks at work, to returning a text message. It is **so** easy to get sidetracked with your mind racing a mind a minute.

16. **Sex Life.** For most, it's more like, *"What sex life?"* But not before long, you learn how to get your timing down packed, how to get your sexy back and how to keep the affection thriving.

As mentioned, designating couple time is the best way to go. Even if couple time is only once a month. Let that one time a month be specifically for your relationship! Call a sitter and plan a date night or quick getaway. Take your partner to his favorite place, or cook his favorite meal. Anything special for the two of you!

Having time set aside to focus on each other strengthens your relationship and whether you know it or not, this is better for baby as well. The more in love you are with one other; the less tension, stress and strain you have on yourself; this increases your overall glee.

17. **Confide in a mommy friend or family member!** You can't do this all on your own! If you try, you will come close to losing your mind! Everything you're experiencing is normal, and if you find someone you **know** you can trust to talk to, you will feel relieved!

There were plenty of times where my best friend and I called each other and wound up saying by the end of the conversation, "WOW! This happened to you too?!" If you feel like pulling out your hair one minute, have anxiety, feeling down, or even if you are in your greatest mood ever-- talk to someone about it! Venting sessions are refreshing!

This also works with basic mommy stories! It is a joy to hear other mom's lives and makes for great play dates! While your children are busy playing, discuss what is going on in your life with baby!

18. **Maintain old friendships!** Before baby joined you in life, you had time for your friends every now

and then-- in most cases, more now than then! It is essential to maintain (**relevant**) friendships!

Relevant friends are those friends who are supportive, trusting, have your best interest at heart and bring out the best in you-- a sisterhood! These friendships are important because they help alleviate anxiety and help you keep a fairly balanced social life.

19. **Talk to your doctor!** This is particularly significant because not only are you reassured that you are completely normal; you hear it from a professional who has plenty of patients and would not steer you in the wrong direction (hopefully).

    Your doctor is there to help, even after birth. They can lend an ear, advice, support, and even link you with another medical professional if they feel you need further aid outside of their spectrum.

20. **Appreciate the [unsolicited] advice!** As soon as the world discovers you are pregnant, in comes the opinions and life theories on everything pregnant from everywhere, even strangers!

    People advise you on what you should do when carrying your baby, how to change baby's diaper, how to breast feed, how to, how to, how to! While some advice can be overwhelming, bombarding, and unwanted, it does prepare you even when it seems that you aren't paying attention.

There were many occasions where I was 'unconsciously' prepared! I noticed how in some situations, I actually took heed to the advice that I thought I ignored. I somehow knew just what to do in areas that I otherwise would have been ill-prepared.

21. **Do not cry over spilled milk (literally!)!** It is so easy to become emotional over the little things, especially if you are running off of two hours of sleep!

    Scenario 1: You wake up in the middle of the night in a scurry to make a bottle, the bottle slips … or maybe you do not have the insert in properly … or perhaps the bottle is not put together correctly; inevitably, milk begins to seep out of the bottle.

    Or,

    Scenario 2: You reach for a diaper inside of your diaper bag, only to discover that everything inside is completely drenched due to baby's bottle not being fastened all the way.

    This can be beyond frustrating, annoying, irritating, and enough to make you break down. But pull it together! Instead of losing it in those moments, remember that you are only human and you are allowed a slip up or three! You are not perfect and no one expects you to be!

Accidents happen; under packing the diaper bag, not having the car seat buckled in properly (I **urge** you to not let this one happen often!), not changing baby's diaper quickly enough, etc. While these moments are extremely trying, remember-- it is all a part of the experience, and believe it or not, as your baby grows, you will appreciate these "oops" moments even more!

22. **It gets easier!** The first couple of months are challenging! This is just the adjustment period for both you and baby! Baby is learning mommy, while mommy is learning baby … and learning how to be a mommy! Though the experience may have its not so great moments, as your baby grows so does your love! You learn so much about you after having a baby that you completely forget about those once rocky moments! As soon as your baby is able to say, "Mommy," it all becomes worthwhile!

23. **For postpartum sufferers.** There is no particular cue as to when the depression will begin or when it will end. My son will be two years old in one week, and I still have my awful moments. I am sure added stresses from outward sources are a

significant factor, but just know that you are not alone. Seeking professional help is key, talking to a friend and even praying about it helps as well. Once you realize/ understand what is going on with you, it becomes easier for you to cope with.

Postpartum depression can affect anyone, and its effects can be detrimental if you do not take control of your symptoms. Speak up and out about your situation. You never know who is suffering with you and may need an ear or helpful words as well.

24. **Put on a happy face!!** Again! This is the greatest experience of your LIFE! Enjoy it! Do not take everything too seriously! Laugh at your mistakes! Have fun being the best mommy you can be!

25. **NO NANNIES ALLOWED!!** I kid! We all need outside help from time to time! However, we are all so very capable of being the mom we dream of to our children! Embrace your new role, both the good and the *bad*, and know that you are only a **real** mom!

Acknowledgements

God: THANK YOU so much for blessing me with the gift of being a mother. This entire experience has been one of the BEST tests/ treats in my life to date!

Parents: <u>Mom</u>; Only the Lord knows where I would be if you weren't able to help and guide me through this process! I was so lost at the beginning, and while at times I thought I had it all figured out, you showed me exactly what I needed to do. For that I am beyond grateful. <u>Dad</u>; Your love towards me from the beginning of my life has shaped me into the woman that I am. I was always the biggest daddy's girl, and for that alone, I never wanted to let you down and it pushed me to be the best Shonda I could be.

Jr.: MOMMY'S HANDSY!!! You're far too young to understand the impact you have had on my life, but it has been the greatest thus far! You've pushed me in ways that I've only dreamed! I'm a better person now, in ways that I thought I was complete, you've made me whole! You've made my soul brave; I feel that I am finally able to take on the world, simply because I have a purpose. YOU! My biggest accomplishment and motivation!

Devin: The greatest best friend/ boyfriend/ everything EVER! You literally helped me through such a hard point of my life without even knowing how bad it was! You've supported me in every dream that I've had, you've pushed me through every fail, you've loved me at times where I know I made it hard, and my love for you is immeasurable!

Jessica: When you asked if I would write this book with you, I was hesitant because as we know, I'm a private person! But the more we shared our mommy experience-- the more I realized we should help others! Thank you for including me in your vision, I wouldn't have <u>ever</u> done this without you!

Taylor: My little big cousin! Thank you for taking such amazing pictures! You rock!! The best is yet to come for you! I love you!

About the Author

LaShonda M. Wilson was born in Washington, DC on October 21, 1985 and has resided in Maryland from the time she was born until the present. After graduating from Hampton University in the Spring of 2007, with a Bachelor's degree in Psychology, she then went on to receive her certificate in Forensic Psychology from The Chicago School of Professional Psychology.

She began contracting for the Department of Defense and United States Agency for International Development; however, LaShonda knew that it was time to follow her passion for entrepreneurship. In this, she began working towards opening her first full service beauty salon at the age of twenty five years old, which she coined, The Plush Salon and Studio, located in her home state of Maryland. Using the Plush name as her inspiration, she also began her own beauty and fashion blog. Notable of her successes and eagerness to help others, she was awarded as a member of the National Association of Professional Women at the age of twenty six years old.

In the midst of this, on July 1, 2010, LaShonda gave birth to a son, whom she calls Jr. During this time, LaShonda "found her ultimate purpose in life," as she describes. In becoming a mother, LaShonda says, "This was one of the biggest challenges of my life; however it has been the most rewarding. My son has pushed me in ways I had never imagined and I only strive to be my best, for him."

www.ingramcontent.com/pod-product-compliance
Lightning Source LLC
LaVergne TN
LVHW011213080426
835508LV00007B/768